This book is dedicated to my family, and especially my grandbabies, and to all the other "tator" tots and princess fluffy toes that I love so much!

© 2022 By Kerry E Garner
7501 E 97th St., Tulsa, OK 74133
All RIGHTS RESERVED
No Reproduction of this work in part or
in whole is given without consent
All stories fictitious, and do not represent any
true person's thoughts, actions or words
ISBN #:979-8-9863470-0-4 paperback
ISBN# 979-8-9863470-1-1 e-book
LCCN # 2022910455
Edition #1
Book 1 of "WITH THE ANIMALS AND ME" Series
ebook, paperback

Kerry E. Garner

ABOUT THE AUTHOR

Kerry E. Garner is an author dedicated to her faith, family, community, and country. Growing up in the beautiful South Arkansas town of Hamburg, Kerry was provided a fertile ground that enriched and nurtured her love of God. She graduated from Oral Roberts University with a degree in English Literature. She married the love of her life, Frank Garner, in 1990, and they raised two incredible sons. Kerry founded a faith-based women's Bible study in 2000, a steadfast endeavor through which she continues to impart the teachings of God to this day. Over the course of two decades, Kerry served her church, offering comfort, encouragement, and a prayer of faith for those in the hospital and those needing altar ministry, where she also served as team lead. Today, she dedicates herself to her family, Ladies' ministry & healing ministry. She attends daily morning prayer at Rhema Bible College and serves as an altar counselor at Victory Church in Tulsa, OK. She continues to study God's word and looks forward to writing more books. Kerry is available for women's ministry speaking engagements and can be contacted at 918-971-8440 or Kerryegarner@gmail.com. Testimonials of breakthrough can be sent to the same email address or sent on messenger to Kerryelisabethgarner on Instagram.

Books by this author can be found on Amazon.com under Kerry E. Garner Books:

A Prayer Warrior's Weapons of War: Rescuing the Lost, Stalked & Prodigals

Children's Book:

The Adventure Series:

Brandon and Brad's Backyard Adventure
Brandon and Brad's Water Park Adventure
Brandon and Brad's Pirate Ship Adventure
Brandon and Brad's Grandparent Adventure
Brandon and Brad's Italian Family's Adventure in Buffalo, NY

With the Animals and Me Series:

Come ABC with the Animals and Me
Come 123 with the Animals and Me
Princess Fluffy Toes Loves to Dance
When Jenny Met Jesus: A Prayer of Salvation for Children
Psalms 23 for Children: Empowered to Face Fears, Bullies, and Life in the Real World

Come ABC

WITH THE ANIMALS AND ME

A a

A is for armadillo,
riding a bike.

B b

B is for bear,
flying a kite!

C c

C is for cat,
counting to two.

D d

D is for duck,
wearing tennis shoes.

E e

E is for eagle,
soaring so high.

F f

F is for fish,
with really big eyes.

G g

G is for giraffe, singing off key!

H h

H is for hippo,
drinking some tea.

I i

I is for iguanas,
running a race.

J j

J is for jellyfish,
making first base.

K k

K is for kangaroo,
trying to fly.

L l

L is for lion,
eating a pie.

M m

M is for monkey,
riding a horse.

N n

N is for narwhal,
at a golf course.

O o

O is for owl,
playing the drum.

P p

P is for porcupine,
chewing some gum.

Q q

Q is for quail,
eating ice cream.

R r

R is for rhino,
on a balance beam.

S s

S is for sheep,
wearing a coat.

T t

T is for tiger,
driving a boat.

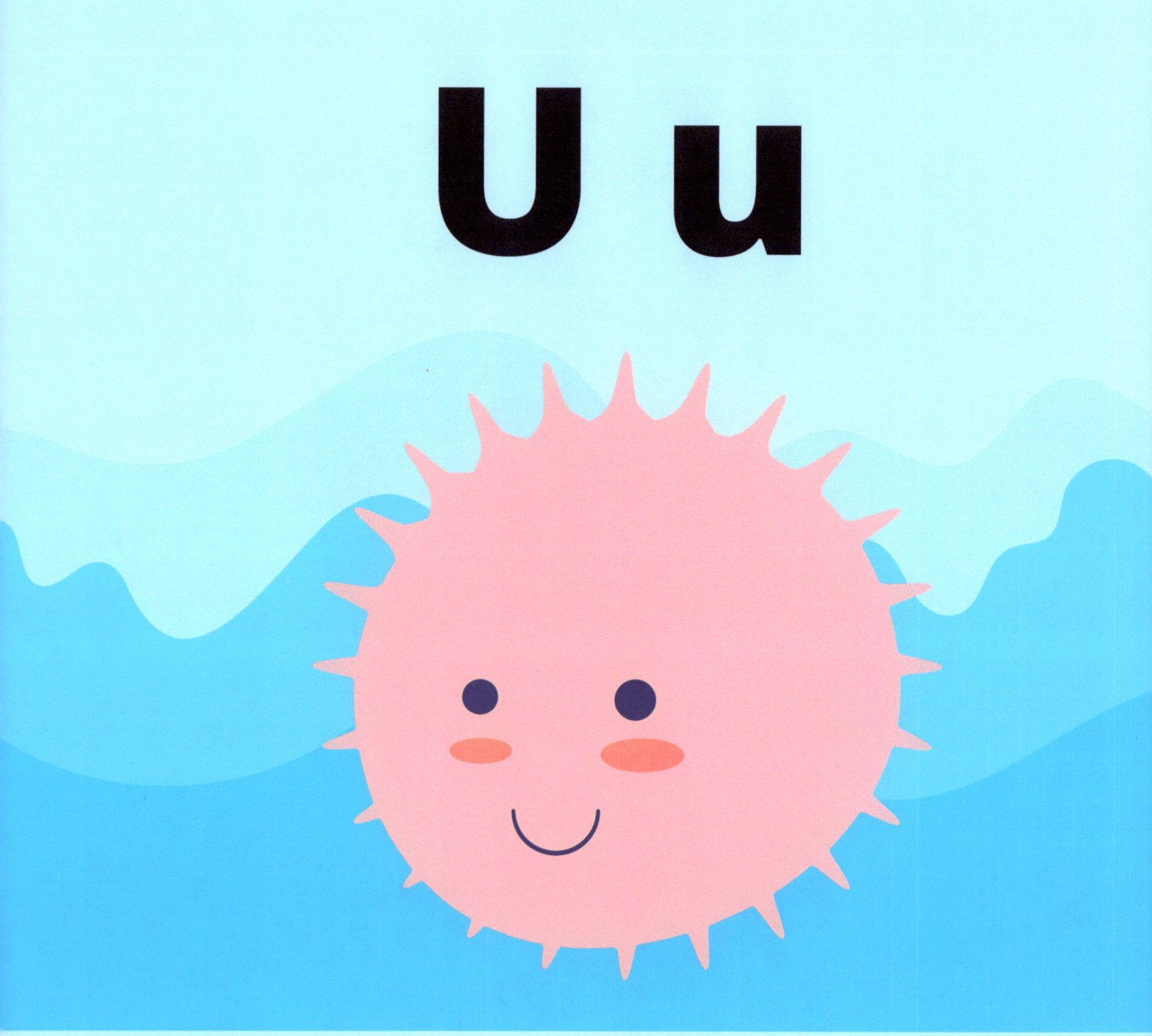

U u

U is for urchin,
that lives in the sea.

V v

V is for vulture,
watching a bee.

W w

W is for worm,
headed to Mars.

X x

X is for xeme,
driving fast cars.

Y y

Y is for yak,
taking a bath.

Z z

Z is for zebra,
making us laugh.

Enjoyed this story? Please leave a review on Amazon and help inspire more adventures!

Amazon.com under Kerry E Garner Books

Go to the link, click the book you are reviewing, then hit "Review this Product" at the very, very bottom.

Thank you!